Ginger and Gem

by Emma Green
illustrated by Holly Jones

Core Decodable 65

Bothell, WA • Chicago, IL • Columbus, OH • New York, NY

MHEonline.com

Copyright © 2015 McGraw-Hill Education

All rights reserved. No part of this publication may be reproduced or distributed in any form or by any means, or stored in a database or retrieval system, without the prior written consent of McGraw-Hill Education, including, but not limited to, network storage or transmission, or broadcast for distance learning.

Send all inquiries to:
McGraw-Hill Education
8787 Orion Place
Columbus, OH 43240

ISBN: 978-0-02-145107-4
MHID: 0-02-145107-9

Printed in the United States of America.

2 3 4 5 6 7 8 9 DOC 20 19 18 17 16 15

Ginger and Gem like this ride.
It is called Space Danger.

Ginger and Gem go up the giant ride.
This stage of the ride is gentle.

Then Ginger and Gem stop.
This is the second stage.

The last stage is a large drop.
Ginger and Gem fall!

Go! Go! Go!
They like this part best!

Ginger and Gem like Space Danger. They will go back.